You and Me

Depend On Me

Angela Leeper

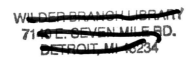
Heinemann Library

Chicago, Illinois

Customer Service 888-454-2279
Visit our website at www.heinemannlibrary.com

Designed by Mike Hogg (Maverick)
Printed and bound in China by South China Printing Company Limited
Photo research by Janet Lankford Moran

09 08 07 06 05
10 9 8 7 6 5 4 3 2 1

Library of Congress Cataloging-in-Publication Data
Leeper, Angela.
   Depend on me / Angela Leeper.
      p. cm. -- (You and me)
   Includes index.
   ISBN 1-4034-6071-X (hardcover) ISBN 1-4034-6079-5 (pbk.)
1. Trust--Miscellanea--Juvenile literature. 2. Reliability--Miscellanea--Juvenile literature. I. Title. II. Series.
   BJ1500.T78L44 2004
   158.2--dc22

                          2004016608

Acknowledgments
The author and publisher are grateful to the following for permission to reproduce copyright material:
Cover photograph by Greg Williams/Heinemann Library
pp. 4, 5, 14, 15, 16, 17 Robert Lifson/Heinemann Library; p. 6 Digital Vision/Getty Images; p. 7 Gabe Palmer/Corbis; pp.
8, 9 Jill Birschbach/Heinemann Library; p. 10 Mary Kate Denny/Photo Edit, Inc.; pp. 11, 18 Warling Studios/Heinemann
Library; p. 12 Royalty-free/Corbis; pp. 13, 19 Michael Newman/Photo Edit, Inc.; pp. 20, 21 QueNet/Heinemann Library;
pp. 22, 23 Janet Moran/Heinemann Library; back cover (L-R) Jill Birschbach/Heinemann Library, Warling
Studios/Heinemann Library

Every effort has been made to contact copyright holders of any material reproduced in this book.
Any omissions will be rectified in subsequent printings if notice is given to the publisher.

Special thanks to our advisory panel for their help in the preparation of this book:

Alice Bethke, Library Consultant
Palo Alto, CA

Eileen Day, Preschool Teacher
Chicago, IL

Kathleen Gilbert,
Second Grade Teacher
Round Rock, TX

Sandra Gilbert,
Library Media Specialist
Fiest Elementary School
Houston, TX

Jan Gobeille,
Kindergarten Teacher
Garfield Elementary
Oakland, CA

Contents

What Is Depending on Someone?

When you depend on someone you trust this person.

You trust this person will finish
a job.

Where Can People Depend on You?

People can depend on you at home.

Your little brother depends on you for help.

People can depend on you
at school.

Your teacher depends on you to
do your own work.

Why Can People Depend on You?

People can depend on you because you are helpful.

They know you will do the job.

People depend on you because
they trust you.

They know you will do your best
to help them.

Who Can Depend on You?

Your parents can depend on you.

They know you will set the table when it is dinnertime.

Your friends can depend on you.

They know you will share and play fair.

What Does It Look Like When People Depend on Each Other?

When someone depends on you, they may see you doing the work.

Your teacher smiles when you finish a job.

What Does It Sound Like When People Depend on Someone?

When you depend on someone you say, "I trust you."

You also may say, "You can do it."

When the job is finished you may say, "Thank you."

You also may say, "Good job!"

How Can People Depend on You at Home?

Your parents depend on you at home.

They trust you to go to school on time.

Your parents depend on you at nighttime.

They trust you to get ready for bed.

How Can People Depend on You at School?

Your teacher depends on you to listen.

Your principal depends on you, too.

He trusts you to follow the school rules.

How Do You Feel When People Depend on You?

When people depend on you, you can feel proud.

You helped finish a job.

You can feel proud because people trust you.

Quiz

Which girl can you depend on to keep her room clean?

Answer to Quiz

You can depend on this child.

She finishes a job.

Note to Parents and Teachers

Reading for information is an important part of a child's literacy development. Learning begins with a question about something. Help children think of themselves as investigators and researchers by encouraging their questions about the world around them. Each chapter in this book begins with a question. Read the question together. Look at the pictures. Talk about what you think the answer might be. Then read the text to find out if your predictions were correct. Think of other questions you could ask about the topic, and discuss where you might find the answers. Assist children in using the picture glossary and the index to practice new vocabulary and research skills.

Index